SNEAKY
ART

For my mother, Joy,
who started me off with scissors and glue

First edition 2013

Library of Congress Catalog Card Number 2012942615
ISBN 978-0-7636-5648-5

LEO 17 16 15 14 13 12
10 9 8 7 6 5 4 3 2 1

Printed in Heshan, Guangdong, China

This book was typeset in PMN Caecilla.
The illustrations were done in cut-paper collage.
Photography and illustrations by Marthe Jocelyn.

Candlewick Press
99 Dover Street
Somerville, Massachusetts 02144

visit us at www.candlewick.com

SNEAKY ART

Crafty Surprises to Hide in Plain Sight

Marthe Jocelyn

CANDLEWICK PRESS

CONTENTS

SNEAKY ART PROJECTS

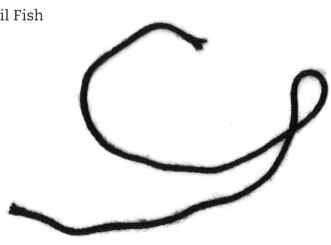

INTRODUCTION

Is there a sneaky artist in you?
Of course there is!

We all like surprises, don't we? Getting and giving
them. This book is a how-to manual for making art
projects from easily found materials. The surprise
comes from where you put your creation. How about
a pair of eyes peeking up from a street grate? Or a
birthday note tied around a tree? Each project is meant
to be displayed in a public place, for people you may or
may not know, in a made-you-look-twice spirit of fun.

The projects suggested in this book are intended as
inspiration to awaken the sneaky artist in you. Once
you get going, you'll have plenty of bright and devious
ideas of your own for how to create art and make
people laugh at the same time.

Remember: Sneaky art is NOT: mean, defacing, ugly, hurtful,
messy, or permanent. Sneaky art is NOT graffiti or
marking up someone else's property.

Sneaky art IS: funny, clever, thoughtful, temporary,
subversive, playful, and surprising!

What are you waiting for? Turn the pages and get
sneaky!

THE SNEAKY ART TOOL KIT

You probably already have most of the tools and materials needed to be a sneaky artist: scissors, glue, tape, twist ties, string, and markers.

The recycling bin can be a treasure trove of other useful items such as magazines, newspapers, greeting cards, wrapping paper, file folders, cereal boxes, juice cartons, and cardboard boxes.

You can find other materials at the craft store or the dollar store—things like construction paper, index cards, other kinds of colored paper, yarn, ribbon, buttons, beads, pipe cleaners, paper plates, and stir sticks.

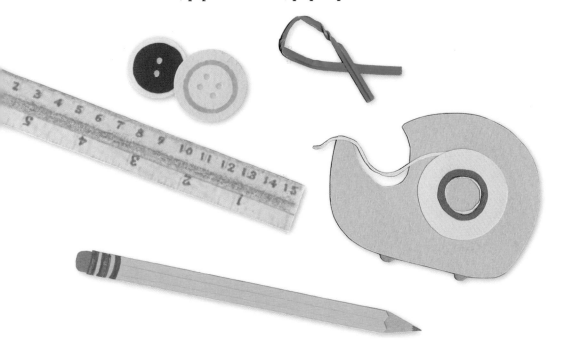

SNEAKY LETTERING

You can use any of FIVE ways to make letters or numbers for the sneaky art projects that call for them:

Write the letters yourself, using a pen, marker, colored pencils, or crayons.

Cut the letters out of magazines.

If you have a set of rubber-stamp letters, use different colored inks or just plain black.

Craft, stationery, and dollar stores sell stencils for letters in an assortment of shapes, styles, and sizes, as well as sticker letters, in many fonts and colors.

I ThiNK YOu WILL LOVe thiS StorY

Once you've decided on the type of letters, make sure the words fit before you glue or ink them in place. Lightly print the letters with a pencil (the same size as the stencils/stickers/stamps that you are using), to measure the available space. If you're making a speech bubble, for instance, write the words before cutting out the bubble shape to make sure there is enough room for everything you want to say.

GOOD Luck!

GETTING SNEAKY!

Once you've finished your art piece, it's time for the sneaky part of the project—the installation. This is usually quick and easy, but it does involve planning ahead and thinking about WHERE, WHEN, and HOW.

Where?   Choosing a sneaky spot will depend on what the project is and whether a place is accessible, safe, and easy to see. Check the weather report if your art will be outdoors. You don't want rain, wind, or snow to ruin the fun.

When?   It helps to know exactly who you want to surprise. A family member? A friend? A stranger? Whoever it is, make sure that person isn't around to see you making your sneaky moves!

If your sneaky art is intended for home, you might have to get up early to install it before anyone else is awake.

If school is the intended location, you'd better get there before your friends or stay a little later in the afternoon. If you've chosen a public place, avoid rush hour!

How?   If you can look at the intended site ahead of time, it will help you plan for installation. Ask yourself these questions: Can the art just sit there safely, or does it need to be attached in some way? Is there a place to tie

(continued)

string? Will tape stick to the surface, or will I need a different method? Do I need to measure anything?

Remember that sneaky art is quick to install and effortless to remove. Nothing should be permanent. If you want to remember how your art looked, snap a photo before sneaking away.

If your art is featured in a public place, check the spot again later. If no one has taken your project, you should reclaim it to use again for another sneak or to exhibit at home.

Don't make anyone mad—make them laugh!

SNEAKY ART PROJECTS

A funny face startles with a smile.

FRACTURED FACES

Where: On a mirror, the refrigerator, a plate, a parking meter, a school locker—or anywhere that sticky notes will stick!

Materials: Old magazines
Sticky notes
Scissors
Glue
For speech bubbles: pen, marker, cut-out letters, or letter stencils; paper

How to Make: 1. Cut lots of different facial features out of magazines. Mismatched eyes and mouths create the funniest faces! And you can always draw your own to add to the collection.

2. Glue the facial features onto individual sticky notes.

3. If you want to include a message, cut out a speech bubble and add cutout or stenciled letters, or simply write your message on a sticky note (see Sneaky Lettering, on page vii, for tips).

How to Sneak: Place the facial features in a plastic folder to transport them to the sneak location. When no one is looking, create your fractured face!

PAPER-PLATE PEEKER

Where: In a window, peering out at the street; in a drawer, cupboard, or refrigerator; in a tree

Materials: Old magazines
Scissors
Paper plates in any solid color
Glue

How to Make:
1. Cut out lots of eyes, noses, mouths, ears, and pieces of hair from pictures in magazines.

2. Play around with the cutouts on a paper plate until you build a face you like.

3. Glue the features in place. Let the face dry.

How to Sneak: The Paper-Plate Peeker can often simply be slipped into a sneaky place, but sometimes it will need securing. Attach it to a window with tape; poke twist ties or string through small holes near the "ears" and tie it to a fence or to the back of a chair. If you hide your peeker in a drawer or cupboard, add a sneaky BOO!

Variations: Use materials other than magazine cutouts, such as buttons, paper scraps, yarn, or your own silly drawings. Build robot faces on aluminum pie tins using old nuts and bolts for the features. You'll need extra-strong glue or craft-glue dots for the metal parts.

A flutter of color turns even a tiny place into a party.

TEENY PARTY

Where: In a medicine cabinet, refrigerator, cupboard, or car; across someone's cubby or computer at school

Materials: Scraps of colored paper, wrapping paper, or magazine pages
Scissors
String, skinny ribbon, dental floss, or fishing line
Glue
Tape for installation (optional)

How to Make: 1. Cut diamond-shaped pieces of paper.

2. The length of string that you cut will be determined by where you plan to install your garland. Be sure to add about 10 inches on each end so you'll have room to tie or tape it in place. It's best to cut a longer piece than you need and trim it later if necessary.

3. Fold each diamond in half, matching the long points, to form a triangle. Crease gently and unfold. Lay flat.

4. Starting about a foot from one end, place the string along the crease line of the first diamond. Put a small dab of glue near the bottom triangle point, then press the two sides together over the string.

(continued)

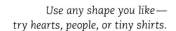

*Use any shape you like—
try hearts, people, or tiny shirts.*

5. Place the next diamond two or three finger-widths over from the first one. Repeat steps 3 and 4 as many times as you need to fill the string, leaving lots of extra for installation at each end.

6. Let dry completely.

7. Store carefully so as not to tangle or mangle before installation.

How to Sneak: The easiest way to install the garland is to tape the ends of the string in place. If tying instead, be sure to tie the ends of the string around two secure places—NOT anything glass and NOT anything that might tip over.

MATCHBOX LULLABY

Where: On a pillow or bedside table, in a purse, or in the glove compartment of a car

Materials: A small matchbox
Medium-weight colored paper
(origami paper works well)
A pencil
Scissors
Old magazines
An index card or card stock
Glue

How to Make:

1. If the box is still holding matches, empty them out and hand them over to an adult

2. Take apart the two pieces of the matchbox. Use the inside section as a pattern, and draw around it onto the back side of the papers you've chosen for the sheet and blanket. Cut them out.

3. Fit the "sheet" into the bottom of the "bed." Trim the "blanket" so that it is slightly smaller and fold one end to look like the edge of a real blanket.

4. For the pillow, cut another piece of paper the same width as your sheet but long enough to roll into a cylinder that tucks neatly into one end of the bed,

(continued)

9

The best surprises often come in small packages.

making sure that it is low enough that the matchbox will still be able to slide shut.

5. To make the outer cover, use the outside section of the matchbox as a pattern, and trace around it on the back side of another piece of colored paper. Flip the box on its side and add the width on either side of your tracing. Cut it out and place it over the outside of the matchbox, folding down the sides.

6. Find a picture of a person or stuffed animal in an old magazine. Cut it out, glue it onto the index card, and trim it around the edges. Alternatively, draw a small character yourself on the card and cut it out.

7. Slip your person or animal under the blanket. Sweet dreams!

How to Sneak: Before bedtime, leave your surprise on someone's pillow or bedside table. You could try it out at home, during a sleepover, or when visiting your grandparents. You can also sneak it into your mother's purse when she isn't looking or hide it in the glove compartment of your family's car.

Variations: Versions of the Teeny Party from page 7 are also fun surprises to hide in a matchbox, especially hearts on Valentine's Day!

This easy garland brings a breath of fresh air to the Laundromat.

TEENSY-WEENSY WASHING LINE

Where: At the Laundromat or in the laundry room of your house or apartment building

Materials: Old clothing catalogs or magazines
Scissors
Index cards or card stock; glue (optional)
Mini clothespins (available at a dollar or craft store)
String, yarn, or dental floss
Tape for installation

How to Make: 1. Cut out pictures of clothes from the catalogs or magazines. It's fine if the sizes do not match perfectly—that's part of the art! If the magazine paper seems flimsy, glue the clothes to index cards. Allow them to dry and then cut around the edge of the garment.

2. Pin the clothes to a length of string

3. You're ready to hang out the washing in a sneaky spot!

How to Sneak: You don't have to attach the line to a washer or a dryer—try hanging it from the shelf where the detergent is kept or along the edge of the laundry basket.

You can also draw, color, and cut out your own clothing designs!

CUP DANGLER

Where: The rim of a coffee or tea mug

Materials: A soft candy fish
A new paper clip

How to Make:
1. Unbend the paper clip into an S shape. Make sure you are using a clean, brand-new paper clip! One end will be the hook while the other will be the hanger.

2. Push the hook end through the mouth area of the candy fish.

3. Hang the other end from the rim of a mug.

How to Sneak: Prepare your fish before you come to the table. Wait until your sneakee isn't looking, and quickly hang your art. Pretend not to notice anything.

Variations: Hang it on a juice glass or cereal bowl instead of a mug. Try it with a soft bear, worm, or other candy shape.

A sweet way to say good morning!

Make your teacher's Monday morning something delicious.

TISSUE-PAPER CUPCAKES

Where: On a teacher's desk, on the seat of your mom's car, inside a mailbox for the mail carrier, or on a friend's desk at school

Materials: Tissue paper in assorted colors
Scissors
Cupcake papers
   (preferably miniature)
Glue
Beads, buttons, and rickrack

Stick a rolled-paper candle into the tissue for a birthday surprise!

How to Make: 1. Cut a piece of tissue paper about the size of a school notebook. Gently crush it into a ball that fits neatly into a cupcake paper.

2. Drizzle glue on the inside bottom of the cupcake paper, and press the tissue ball in place.

3. To decorate the cupcake, you can: Dot glue on the tissue ball and sprinkle on colored beads. Glue on several little buttons, or maybe just one big one. Glue on a rim of rickrack to look like fancy frosting. Tightly roll scraps of tissue paper—brown for chocolate chips or red for bits of fruit.

How to Sneak: If your treat is for a teacher or a friend at school, get to school early to put the cupcake on a napkin or a paper plate and leave it for the lucky recipient. Will you leave a message or be a secret chef?

Sail to sea in a fountain or a sink.

SINK BOATS

Where: In a bathroom sink or public fountain

Materials: Two corks (If no one drinks wine at your house,
restaurants are usually happy to save corks for
a young artist in the neighborhood. Craft-supply
stores also sell corks by the bag.)
Glue, preferably not water-soluble
Wooden or plastic stir sticks
A juice or milk carton
   (washed and dried)
Scissors
A thick rubber band
A hole punch
Food coloring
   (optional for sink installation)

*You can also make your
boat out of Styrofoam!*

How to Make: 1. Dribble glue along one side of each cork. Place the
end of a stir stick between them (to act as the mast),
and press together. This is where you'll need patience:
allow the glue to dry fully (even overnight) before
proceeding. A rubber band works well as a clamp—
or even a permanent fixture—to keep the corks
together.

2. Cut out a triangular sail from the juice or milk carton.
Punch a hole (or cut a small slit) half an inch from the
top of the sail, and a second hole half an inch from
the bottom edge.

(continued)

3. Poke the stir stick through the hole at the bottom of the sail and then through the hole at the top. The stiffness of the board should keep the sail in place.

4. Cut a small flag out of any paper and glue it to the top of the mast.

How to Sneak: You'll have to be the first person in the bathroom if you plan to turn the sink into a harbor, and be sure to brush your teeth before you get started! If your chosen sneaky spot is a public fountain, launch your boat quickly when no one is watching, and hope for smooth sailing. . . .

Variations: If corks are not available, here are two other options:

Styrofoam Sailboat:

1. Glue together four layers cut from a Styrofoam produce tray. Allow to dry fully.

2. Make the sail and mast as in steps 2 and 3 above.

3. Poke your mast through the Styrofoam layers as deep as it will go. Remove the mast, put a drop or two of glue in the hole, and replace the mast. Allow to dry.

Flat-Bottom Boat:

1. Cut off the bottom inch of a milk or juice carton (or cut an individual juice box in half lengthwise). You'll need a blob of putty or chewing gum in the center of the deck to secure the mast.

SEEING RED

Where: Anywhere outside that needs brightening

Materials: Red ribbon, pipe cleaners, or yarn

How to Make: Here are some suggestions for ways to dot the world with sneaky little spots of red:

Red ribbon tied in bows in unexpected places—around a tree branch before new leaves have grown in the spring or around the door handle of a car.

Red pipe cleaners with twirled ends, bunched and fastened around a parking meter.

A single piece of red yarn attached to one end of a long fence and woven in and out as far as you can go, or taped occasionally along the top edge.

How to Sneak: Avoid busy times in the park or the street whenever you plan to install something sneaky—or red. Leave behind something pretty and bright where a passerby will least expect it, something to make heads turn and eyes look twice.

(continued)

A bright red spot in a dull place will always be eye-catching.

Variations: A colorful yarn cozy can cheer up signposts, park benches, bicycle racks, tree trunks, and branches. Make several braids of yarn, using red with two other colors. Fasten them all together with twist ties, creating tassels at the end of each braid. Now you have enough to wrap around anything that needs warming up! Wait for a chance to install your art carefully, in peace. A Yarn Fest can take a few minutes to get right. Roll the braid into a ball so you can hold it in one hand. Wrap the braid around the branch or post, keeping the loops snug with each other. Tuck in the ends or let them dangle.

FINGERS AND TOES

Where: On a chair or doorknob

Materials: Outgrown baby socks
An old single glove, preferably child-size
Stuffing material such as newspaper, toilet paper,
or tissue paper

How to Make a Chair Footer:

1. Slip socks onto the feet of a chair. No need to match or fasten!

How to Make a Glove Greeter:

1. Scrunch up bits of your stuffing material, and stuff it into the glove until it stands up on its own. Leave space for the doorknob!

2. Slide the wrist of the glove over a doorknob. Adjust stuffing amount if necessary.

How to Sneak: Slip the socks onto the chair legs before anyone else enters the room. Try to install your friendly handshake when no one is inside so it is there to say hello when someone comes home.

Variations: Chairs in the classroom, dining room, or office. Rubber gloves or gardening gloves on an outdoor faucet, bicycle handles, a grandparent's walker, or the gearshift of a car.

Do household objects get cold hands and feet?

Let other giants discover
your miniature world.

LITTLE LANDMARKS

Where: At the base or among the roots of trees on city streets, in public gardens, or at the playground

Materials: Small boxes such as jewelry boxes, matchboxes, or empty juice boxes
Small stones as weights (optional)
Scraps of different papers such as brown craft paper, newspapers, wrapping paper, or origami paper
Scissors
Glue

How to Make: 1. If you want to place a stone inside your box as a weight against wind, do that first. Then wrap each box as if it were a present, and glue the wrapping in place. Using different colored papers, cut out a roof, windows, and doors and glue them in place.

2. Make buildings in lots of different shapes and sizes to create an intriguing civilization!

How to Sneak: As always, scout out the location ahead of time, arrive prepared, and work fast. Check the weather report before you install your Little Landmarks—you don't want them flooded by rain or snowed under. And avoid leaving them where a dog might pee!

Create tiny worlds inside, too.

PICK ME UP!

Leave a penny on the ground.
Spread the lucky day around!

LUCKY PENNY

Where: On the floor of a store or a bank, in a parking lot, or in the hall at school

Materials: A colored index card or card stock
Scissors — with decorative blades if available
A shiny penny
Tape, double-sided tape, or putty
Lettering materials: markers, cutout letters and glue, letter stencils, rubber stamps, or stickers

How to Make: 1. Cut out a card for the penny in any shape you like.

2. Tape the penny onto the card.

3. Write a lucky message using marker, cutout letters, or stenciled letters. Here are some suggestions:

Good Luck Today!

Lucky Tuesday!

Pick Me Up!

Share the Luck!

How to Sneak: Make sure no one is watching, and leave the penny where someone is sure to find it! You can also slip a penny card into the backpack or lunch box of a friend who has a big test or needs extra luck for whatever reason.

You will learn a secret!

FORTUNE COOKIES

Where: In a lunch box, in the cafeteria, on a teacher's desk, or as party favors

Materials: Cupcake papers, any color
Glue
Plain paper, any color
Scissors
Pen or marker

How to Make:

1. Fold—but do not crease—a cupcake paper so that it forms a half-moon. Put a dot of glue in the center of the curved edge to stick the edges together. Hold the glued spot together until it's dry.

2. Holding the glued place with one hand, gently push in the middle of the bottom of the cupcake paper so that it folds in to form a crescent. Put another dot of glue between the two sides and press together.

3. For each cookie, cut a strip of paper about half an inch wide and four inches long. Write a fortune on each strip.

4. Slide the fortune into the cookie.

How to Sneak: These paper cookies are even more fragile than the real thing, so choose your sneaky spot with care, and consider how the art will be transported. A plastic food container should protect them from being crushed. Leave the cookies in an open place, on a napkin or paper plate.

Brighten someone's day
with an unexpected gift (tag).

TAGLINES

Where: On the bus or subway, on a fence or parking meter, near a water fountain, on a friend's locker or the back of his or her chair, inside the family car, or on a doorknob

Materials: String tags—either purchased (from an office supply store), or homemade with heavyweight paper such as poster board, old file folders, or index cards

For homemade tags:
Scissors
A hole punch
Reinforcements (optional)
String or yarn

Lettering materials: Pen, markers, cutout letters and glue, letter stencils, rubber stamps, or stickers

How to Make: 1. For homemade tags, cut out any shape you like. Just make sure it's big enough to fit your message. Punch a hole at one end, not too close to the edge. Thread a 4-inch length of string through the hole, and knot the ends together, creating a loop.

2. Add a cheerful greeting or funny phrase.

How to Sneak: Turn routine moments or ordinary objects into bright spots. Sneak a tag onto the steering wheel before the morning commute, or attach one to a friend's backpack before dismissal.

Variations: Glue on colorful shapes or decorations. Make a tag shaped like a flower, a bug, or a star.

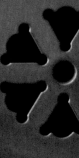

POST A POEM

Where: On a friend's locker, a park bench, a window, a mailbox, or anywhere sticky notes will stick

Materials: Sticky notes
Lettering materials: Pen, markers, cutout letters and glue, letter stencils, rubber stamps, or stickers
Plastic file folder for transportation (optional)

How to Make:

1. Think about words you like and words that sound good together.

2. Make lots of single-word sticky notes, using any or all of the lettering methods described on page viii. The more variety, the better!

3. You might want to write your poem in a notebook first so you can be sure to have all the words ready to sneak. If you prefer to improvise on the spot, remember to make a few words that will connect your more poetic choices, such as *and, you, will, be, a, to, can,* and others.

How to Sneak: As an undercover poet, carry a plastic folder with a choice of words so you will never lose your voice!

Mix up words to make poetry, or just post a message loud and clear.

Put on wings or a crown and you've made a little magic.

STICK PIXIES

Where: At a restaurant, in a teacher's pencil can, or in a kitchen utensil jar

Materials: Old magazines or copies of family photographs
Scissors
Index cards or card stock
Glue, tape
Colored paper, newspaper, feathers, doilies
Craft sticks, stir sticks, or straws

How to Make:
1. Cut out faces from old magazines or copies of family photos, leaving extra room around the edges.

2. Glue the photo onto an index card, and allow it to dry completely. This will make the character sturdier and less likely to get torn.

3. While the glue is drying, cut out wings, a hat, or a crown. Add other scraps or trimmings.

4. Once the glue is dry, trim around the picture again, this time as closely as you can without nipping off an ear.

5. Glue or tape on the wings, hat, or crown.

6. Tape the character to a stick.

How to Sneak: Carry pixies in a folder in your backpack, ready for last-minute drops into sneaky habitats. As easy as grabbing a spoon for hot chocolate or borrowing a pencil, you can leave a Stick Pixie behind.

CORK CRITTERS

Where: At the grocery store or in houseplants

Materials: Corks
Scraps of fabric or paper
Scissors
Glue
Markers

How to Make: Using tiny scraps and bits, along with your imagination, glue on ears, eyes, a nose, hair, and some fashion details.

How to Sneak: Offer to help with the grocery shopping, and then be extra-sneaky, slipping a critter or two onto shelves or among the vegetables.

Variations: Paper People! Instead of corks, make your own little cylinders out of index cards. Decorate as you would a cork, with odd, tiny scraps.

Friendlier than mice, these critters peek out from hiding to say hello.

Pass along the word about
your favorite book!

LIBRARY SHOUTS

Where: Tucked into books at a library or bookstore

Materials: Card stock

Scissors

Lettering materials: Pen, markers, cutout letters, letter stencils, rubber stamps, or stickers

Glue (optional)

How to Make: 1. Cut out speech or thought bubbles from the card stock.

2. Add your message. Keep it short!

3. If you've used glue, press the speech bubble under something heavy so it dries flat. When the lettering is complete, you can also add pictures or decorations.

How to Sneak: Tuck the shouts into books you really like and want to share with others.

These simple puppets are willing messengers.

FILTER FELLOWS

Where: In a library or bookstore, at school, on a wooden spoon or detergent bottle in the kitchen

Materials: Cone-shaped coffee filters (not basket filters)
Markers

How to Make: 1. Draw a face on a coffee filter. You can make it simple, with just a few quick lines, or extra-fancy.

How to Sneak: This is one of the quickest sneaks of all! These fellows slide easily between the books on a shelf or slip over all kinds of ordinary objects to create kooky characters.

A flash of color makes the spirit soar
wherever it alights.

CLIP-ON FLOCK

Where: On tree branches, in houseplants, or on wire fences

Materials: Red card stock (and other colors for variations)
Scissors
Glue
Clothespins

How to Make: 1. Cut out a bird shape. (Find some patterns on the endpapers.)

2. If you like, cut out a wing shape in a different color and glue it into place.

3. Glue the bottom edge of the bird to the narrow side of a clothespin, avoiding the hinge.

4. Let it dry completely.

How to Sneak: Just clip it on anywhere and sneak away.

Variations: Cardinals are not the only creatures that work for this project. Blue jays, robins, insects, butterflies, pixies, or your own imaginary animals could also brighten a gray branch.

Try clipping a flock onto the carts at the grocery store!

Motion is a partner in making this art dance.

SWINGLES

Where: On the swings at the playground

Materials: Crepe-paper streamers in a variety of bright colors
Scissors
Colored duct tape (packing tape or masking tape works
  well, too)
A hole punch
String—2 lengths about 24 inches each

How to Make: 1. Cut several two-foot-long strips of crepe-paper
streamers.

2. Cut a piece of tape about 14 to 16 inches long. Lay it
on your worktable, sticky side up.

3. Place the crepe paper strips along the middle of the
tape. Fold the tape lengthwise over the paper ends
to form the top of the Swingle.

4. Punch a hole in each end of the tape. Thread string
through the hole, and knot it, leaving about a foot
to use for installation.

How to Sneak: Make sure someone is holding the swing for you if you
are standing on the seat to tie the Swingle in place.

Variations: Attach sound makers—such as jingle bells, metal rings,
or seashells—that will ring or clink when the wind
blows. Try it with strips of newspaper.

Flowers brighten any day, but especially one with gray skies and snow.

WINTER BLOSSOMS

Where: Strung from bare or snowy branches

Materials: A variety of colored index cards or milk or juice cartons
Scissors
Yarn
A darning needle (with an eye large enough to thread yarn)

How to Make:

1. Cut out several blossom and leaf shapes. (Find some patterns on the endpapers.)

2. Cut a piece of yarn or string, whatever length you like, maybe using your own height as a measurement.

3. Tie a knot in one end of the yarn. Thread the other end though the eye of the darning needle.

4. Poke the needle through the center of a blossom, and push the blossom down the yarn to about four inches from the knot.

5. Continue to string the blossoms, pulling them gently into place, evenly distributing them along the yarn, which will be thick enough to hold them snugly.

6. When you've finished stringing the blossoms, tie a knot in the top end.

Where to Sneak: Tie your blossom string in a place that people pass often, somewhere especially dulled by winter, so your art will make the moment bloom with cheer.

PAINTED STONES

Where: At a park, in a garden, or at a beach

Materials: Smooth stones
White correction fluid

How to Make:

1. Make sure the stones are clean and dry before you begin.

2. Bottles of correction fluid come with brushes or foam tips—this makes for easy painting on stones. Eyes, nose, mouth, hair—you know how to draw a face!

How to Sneak: You can carry a little bottle of correction fluid when you go to the beach, or you can collect stones to paint at home and redistribute in sneaky places.

You can also wrap stones with colorful yarn or bright ribbons.

Add a face to make an ordinary stone stand out.

Create a school of glimmering silver
fish swimming along the sand!

TINFOIL FISH

Where: At a beach or in a sandbox

Materials:
Card stock
Scissors
Tinfoil
Colored markers
Sticks
Tape

How to Make:

1. Cut out a fish shape from the card stock. Tear a piece of tinfoil that is twice as wide and long as your fish.

2. Crinkle the foil gently, then smooth it back out. The surface will be creased and scaly-looking.

3. Loosely wrap the fish shape with the foil, shiny side out. Shape it by rolling the edges and pinching it to fit around the fins and tail.

4. Tint the scales using the markers. Draw on the eye (or cut and glue on a small black circle).

5. Make a few fish and bring them, along with a roll of tape, to the beach or park. Find some sticks and tape the fish to them.

How to Sneak: Push the sticks into the sand.

Variations: Don't stop at flat fish! Try making three-dimensional sea life or other animals, too.

YOU'VE MADE SOME TERRIFIC ART and put it in
clever places. You've installed surprises without being seen or
damaging anyone's property. Now comes the tricky part: you
have to leave it there and go on your way! In some cases, you
can spy on the people you intended to find your art, but often
you will be elsewhere when their smiles appear or when they
turn sneaky, too, and take your project home. Although it's hard
to leave behind a treasure that you're proud of, you can always
make another work of art, maybe even sneakier next time. . . .